Baby Animals!

By Ruth Thomson

Pictures by Ian Fry

Gareth Stevens Publishing
Milwaukee

BRIGHT IDEA BOOKS:

First Words!
Picture Dictionary!
Opposites!
Sounds!

The Four Seasons!
Pets and Animal Friends!
The Age of Dinosaurs!
Baby Animals!

Mouse Count!
Time!
Animal 1*2*3!
Animal ABC!

Homes Then and Now!
Other People, Other Homes!

Library of Congress Cataloging-in-Publication Data

Thomson, Ruth.
  Baby animals!

  (Bright idea books)
  Bibliography: p.
  Includes index.
  Summary: Introduces baby animals of Africa, the polar ice caps, and North America. Suggests activities for readers to find out more about non-domestic animals.
  1. Animals—Infancy—Juvenile literature.
[1. Animals—Infancy] I. Fry, Ian, ill. II. Title.
QL763.T47 1985   591.3'9   85-25443
ISBN 0-918831-70-9
ISBN 0-918831-69-5 (lib. bdg.)

This North American edition first published in 1985 by

Gareth Stevens, Inc.
7221 West Green Tree Road   Milwaukee, Wisconsin 53223, USA

U.S. edition, this format, copyright © 1985
Supplementary text copyright © 1985 by Gareth Stevens, Inc.
Illustrations copyright © 1984 by Octopus Books Limited

First published in the United Kingdom with an original text copyright by Octopus Books Limited.

Typeset by Ries Graphics, Ltd.
Series Editors: MaryLee Knowlton and Mark J. Sachner
Cover Design: Gary Moseley
Reading Consultant: Kathleen A. Brau

Contents

Baby Animals of the African Plains

The plains of Africa are hot and dusty. The animals rest in the shade of trees and bushes.

Young elephants, giraffes, and chimpanzees learn to eat trees and bushes.

Young lions learn to hunt for their food.

The games of the baby animals help them learn about life on the plains.

Elephants

Elephants live in family groups of mothers and their calves.

This mother takes good care of her calf. She shades it from the sun, protects it from hyenas, and strokes it with her trunk. If the calf doesn't behave, she may slap it with her trunk!

This mother squirts her baby, first with water, and then with dust. The dust protects it from insects and the sun.

This calf learns how to find food. Its mother holds down a high branch, and the calf twists it off.

When these calves are older, they enjoy squirting each other. Elephants love to bathe!

Lions

Lions live in groups called prides. Most prides have two male lions and three or more female lions and their cubs. The adults take turns watching the cubs.

Lion cubs cannot see or walk when they are born. Their mother moves them safely from bush to bush. This is how she protects them from leopards and hyenas.

Young cubs are very playful. Older cubs
hunt with their mother. They learn to
crouch and stay still, and they share the
food she catches.

Giraffes

Baby giraffes are born one at a time. At first, the baby feeds only on its mother's milk. But soon, it eats whatever its mother eats. This is how it learns about the best plants.

If a lion comes near, the baby hides under its mother. She kicks at the lion with her front legs.

To drink, this baby giraffe spreads its front legs. Then it stretches its long neck. One day, it will be as graceful as its mother!

SOUTH SHORE
HERBSTER
H-86-555

11

Chimpanzees

Chimpanzees love trees. They sleep there at night and rest from the sun there during the day. Even their favorite foods — leaves, fruit, bark, and seeds — come from the trees!

This mother carries her baby everywhere she goes. Older chimps also carry the younger ones and protect them from harm.

Chimps are really very clean! They like to pick seeds from each other's fur.

Baby Animals of the North American Woods

The woods are full of animal life. Deer seek shelter among the trees. Foxes roam, looking for food.

Squirrels build nests high in the branches. Frogs lounge around the ponds.

In the woods, baby animals learn the ways of their kind.

15

Deer

The mother deer goes into the woods to have her baby. There, she has the baby in a soft, quiet spot. The new baby is called a fawn.

The fawn peacefully drinks its mother's milk.

The fawn's coat is soft and spotty. The spots make it hard for other animals to see it in the woods.

When the fawn is older, it joins the herd with its mother. She barks to protect it from danger. The fawn crouches low.

This male deer is one year old. He is called a yearling. When he is older, the two knobs on his head will grow into horns.

Foxes

Fox cubs are born in a den. This den is called an earth. The mother feeds the cubs with her milk.

When the cubs are few weeks old, their mother takes them out to play. She now feeds them food scraps.

These cubs are playing hunting games. One cub flicks its tail, and the other pounces on it.

Bigger cubs learn to
hunt food for
themselves. They
pounce on beetles
and worms.

Their mother brings them
food until they are old
enough to find their own.
She also teaches them
what food is good to eat.

Squirrels

Squirrels are born blind and hairless. Their home is a safe, cozy nest called a drey.

The babies stay warm in the drey for several weeks. If there is danger nearby, their mother carries them away.

These young squirrels chase each other for fun.

Once they leave the nest, young squirrels find food for themselves.

They also keep each other clean.

Frogs

This frog has just laid her eggs in the pond. The eggs are covered with jelly. This protects them and keeps them warm.

In a few weeks, tiny tadpoles hatch. They look like fish with tails, and they eat water plants. They eat and eat and grow and grow.

Now its tail is almost gone! The little frog jumps out of the water. Then it hops off into the tall, damp grass.

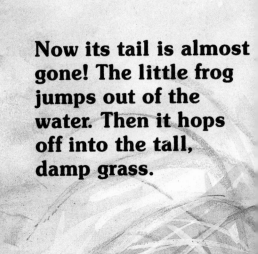

Now its front legs are longer. Its tail is getting shorter. Now it looks more and more like a frog.

The back legs of this tadpole have started to grow.

Baby Animals of the Polar Ice Caps

The ice caps of the north and south polar seas are cold and lonely. But many animals make their homes here.

Polar bears live in the Arctic north. Penguins live in the southern half of the world.

Seals and whales live in the cold, too. But sometimes they swim to warmer waters.

These baby animals live in a frozen world of ice and snow.

Polar Bears

In autumn, a mother bear digs a den in a snowdrift. Here, in deepest winter, her twin cubs are born. She cuddles them for warmth. She feeds them with her milk.

In spring, the hungry mother comes out of her den. The cubs follow close behind.

The cubs slide in the snow while their mother looks for food.

The mother scoops for fish
from the water with her paw.

The cubs follow their mother
everywhere. They learn to hunt by
copying every move she makes.

Penguins

Penguins nest together in a place called a rookery. Their nest is lined with stones to keep the eggs in place.

This chick keeps warm under its mother.

This chick reaches right inside its father's throat for the food he has brought!

Older chicks huddle in groups. An adult watches them very carefully.

Their feathers have grown. Now the young penguins leave home to waddle to the sea.

Seals

Seal pups are born in the spring on the frozen Arctic ice.

The pup feeds on its mother's milk. Soon it has a layer of fat to keep it warm. This fat is called blubber.

The mother is always nearby to protect her pup from harm.

Older pups lose their long, white coats. Now they have short, gray, spotted fur. And now they eat shrimp and squid on the cold Arctic ice.

Soon the pups swim well and grow strong teeth. Now they will follow their mother north and eat fish all summer long.

Whales

Whales find their food in the sea. A favorite food is krill, which are tiny sea animals like shrimp.

Here is a mother fin whale of the polar seas. She has swum to warm waters to give birth to her calf.

After the whale calf is born, its mother pushes it to the top. Now it can breathe air. The mother feeds the calf underwater, however. She squirts her milk into its mouth.

The calf stays near its mother.
Sometimes sharks and other whales
swim too close. Then she splashes her
tail in the water to scare them away.

Baby Animals of the North American Skies

Creatures of the air make their homes everywhere.

Eagles live high in the mountains.

Sparrows live in fields, towns, and even cities.

Honeybees live in honeycombs that hang in the trees.

Butterflies live among the flowers.

Everywhere we look,
birds and insects are
busy with their lives
in the air.

Eagles

Eagles build their nest high on a cliff. Every year, they come back to their nest. First they fix it up with sticks and soft leaves. Then the mother lays her eggs.

The mother shelters the chick from the sun and the rain and the cold.

This eaglet is flying for the first time. Right now, its parents still bring it food. But soon, it will learn to hunt for itself.

The father hunts for food to give the chick. When the chick is very young, the father feeds it with his mouth.

Sparrows

Sparrows build a nest of straw and soft feathers. Often, they build their nest in a crack in a wall.

The parents hunt for food all day long. When the chicks hear their parents coming, they chirp loudly.

Sparrows splash in puddles to keep clean.

Watch out for cats!

This young sparrow
has left the nest. But it
doesn't know how to
find food yet. Its
parents feed it right
out of their mouths.

Honeybees

Honeybees live in a honeycomb.

It is made up of wax cells. Each cell has six sides.

Each honeycomb has only one queen bee. She spends all her time laying eggs. Worker bees clean her and feed her.

The queen lays one egg in each cell.

An egg hatches into a larva in three days. The larva is like a worm and has no wings. Worker bees feed the larva.

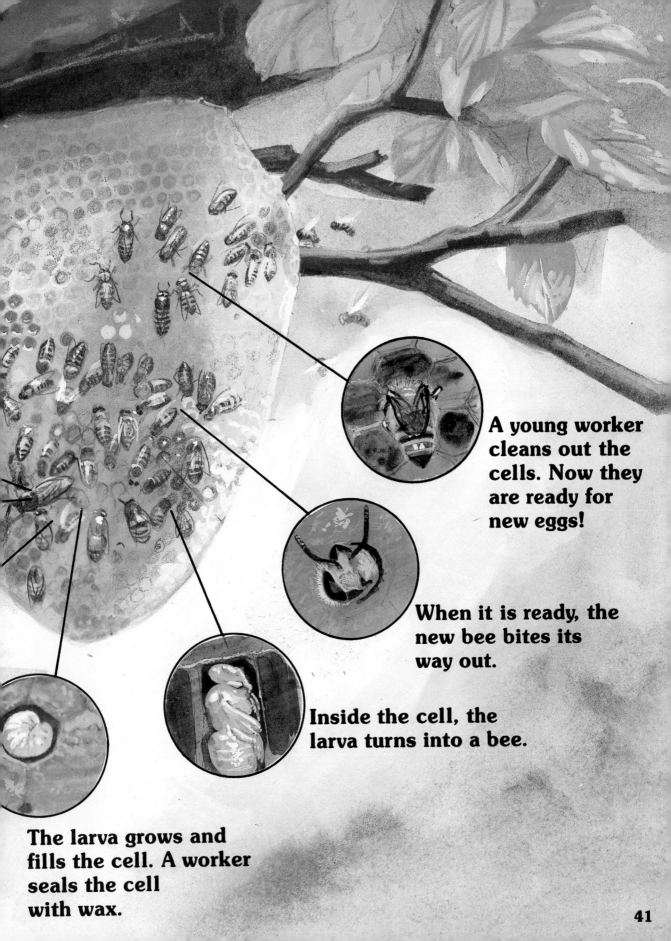

A young worker
cleans out the
cells. Now they
are ready for
new eggs!

When it is ready, the
new bee bites its
way out.

Inside the cell, the
larva turns into a bee.

The larva grows and
fills the cell. A worker
seals the cell
with wax.

Butterflies

All summer, butterflies dance in the air. They sip sweet juice called nectar from flowers with their long tongues.

This butterfly lays her eggs one by one on a plant. The eggs hatch as caterpillars. Then the caterpillars eat the plant!

The caterpillar eats
and eats and grows
larger and larger.

When the caterpillar is
fully grown, it sheds
its skin. Then it grows
a hard cover over its
body. It stays this way
all winter.

In spring, a pretty
butterfly breaks out
and flies off!

43

The following "Things to Talk About," "Things to Do," and "Index of Animal Names" offer grown-ups suggestions for further activities and ideas for young readers of *Baby Animals!*

Things to Talk About

1. Imagine that you are a teacher giving a report or telling a story! Tell what the mother polar bear does in each of the three seasons on pages 26 and 27.

2. On page 43, we learn about the hard covering a caterpillar grows. Do you know what that covering is called?

3. What other insect besides a butterfly grows a covering like that?

4. Use the Index of Animal Names to find the pages about fawns. Does it surprise you to learn that a mother deer barks to protect her fawn? Why?

   What sound did you think a deer might make?

5. Let's go back to the mother polar bear! Were you surprised to learn that she stays in her den all winter long? Why?

   Do you know the word we use to mean sleeping all winter long? If you don't, ask a grown-up you know to talk about this with you.

Things to Do

1. What animals can you think of to put into each of these lists? Use the Index of Animal Names on page 46 for animal names to choose from.
   - Animals that swim.
   - Animals that eat insects.
   - Animals that live in the trees.
   - Animals that make their own homes.
   - Animals that live both in water and on land.

2. Now make a list of the baby names of these animals: *deer, *lion, *fox, *whale, *eagle, *elephant, *seal, *penguin, *bee, *butterfly, *frog.

   What is special about baby butterflies and frogs that make them different from other baby animals? Draw a picture of each of these special baby animals.

3. Here are some things you can do at the zoo. You can also do these things in the woods or near your apartment or house.
   - Pick out some baby animals that interest you, like lion cubs, baby monkeys, rabbits, or puppies.
   - What do the mother animals do to take care of their babies?
   - What kinds of games do you see the babies playing?
   - How might their games help them live in an outdoor home or outside of the zoo?

4. You can read about these babies in this book and in other books from the library. You can also talk to other people about what you've found out.

Index of Animal Names

More Books About Baby Animals

Here are some more books about baby animals. Look
at the list. If you see any books you would like to read,
see if your library or bookstore has them.

*All Wild Creatures Welcome: The Story of a Wildlife
    Rehabilitation Center.* Curtis (Lodestar)
Amazing Facts About Animals. Craig (Doubleday)
Animal Babies. McNaught (Random House)
Baby Animals. Burton (Sunflower)
Farm Babies. Freedman (Holiday House)
Favorite Wild Animals of North America. Vandivert
    (Random House)
How Kittens Grow. Selsam (Scholastic Book Service)
How Puppies Grow. Selsam (Scholastic Book Service)
How to Draw Baby Animals. Sonkin (Troll)
Last Puppy. Asch (Prentice-Hall)
Little Duck. Dunn (Random House)
Little Kitten. Dunn (Random House)
Little Lamb. Dunn (Random House)
Little Rabbit. Dunn (Random House)
Little Raccoon. Noguere (Holt, Rinehart & Winston)
Little Wild Elephant. Michel (Pantheon)
Little Wild Lion Cub. Michel (Pantheon)
Mammals. Zim (Golden Press)
Night and Day. Ribley (Goldencraft)
Nine True Dolphin Stories. Davidson (Scholastic
    Book Service)
Snow Babies. Kassian (Goldencraft)
Who Lives Here. Barlowe (Random House)
Wild Orphan Babies: Mammals and Birds. Weber
    (Holt, Rinehart & Winston)

For Grown-ups

Baby Animals! is a picture book that introduces young readers to baby animals of Africa, the polar ice caps, and North America. The "Index of Animal Names" on page 46 gives educators, librarians, and parents a quick guide to using this book to complement and challenge a young reader's developing language and reading skills.

The editors invite interested adults to examine the sampling of reading level estimates below. Reading level estimates help adults decide what reading materials are appropriate for children at certain grade levels. These estimates are useful because they are usually based on syllable, word, and sentence counts — information that is taken from the text itself.

As useful as reading level scores are, however, we have not slavishly followed the dictates of readability formulas in our efforts to encourage young readers. Most reading specialists agree that reading skill is built on practice in reading, listening, speaking, and drawing meaning from language — activities that adults "do" when they read with children. These factors are not measured by readability scores; and yet they do enhance a text's value and appeal for children at early reading levels.

In *Baby Animals!*, the "Contents," "Things to Talk About," "Things to Do," index, and "More Books to Read About Baby Animals" sections help children become good readers by encouraging them to <u>use</u> the words they read as conveyors of meaning, not as objects to be memorized. And these sections give adults a chance to participate in the learning — and fun — to be found in this story.

Reading level analysis: SPACHE 3.1, FRY 2, FLESCH 97 (very easy), RAYGOR 3, FOG 4, SMOG 2